IMAGES
of America

ST. SIMONS ISLAND

ARCHITECTURAL DRAWING OF ST. SIMONS LIGHTHOUSE, 1867. This plan for a Third Order Lighthouse was drawn under the direction of Brig. Gen. O.M. Poe.

IMAGES
of America

St. Simons Island

Patricia Morris

ARCADIA
PUBLISHING

Published by Arcadia Publishing
Charleston, South Carolina

Library of Congress Catalog Card Number: 2003111111

For all general information contact Arcadia Publishing at:
Telephone 843-853-2070
Fax 843-853-0044
E-mail sales@arcadiapublishing.com
For customer service and orders:
Toll-Free 1-888-313-2665

Visit us on the Internet at www.arcadiapublishing.com

CONTENTS

Acknowledgments 6

Foreword 7

1. A Summer Retreat: Native Americans and St. Simons Island 9

2. The British and the Settlement of Fort Frederica 15

3. St. Simons Island Plantations 25

4. Aids to Navigation: The St. Simons Island Light Station 45

5. The Lumber Mills 61

6. The Military Comes to St. Simons 73

7. Tourism: New Growth for the Island 95

ACKNOWLEDGMENTS

The photographs in this volume are from the collection of the Coastal Georgia Historical Society, repository for Glynn County, Georgia. It is important to thank the staff and the volunteers of the society, especially Bonnie Hendrix and Ed Ginn, for their help and assistance. This book is dedicated to the memory of Martha Morris (Grammy) and my parents, Victor and Constance Hardy.

FOREWORD

Most of us have a healthy curiosity about the place we live. Who dwelled here before us 50, 100, 200 years ago? What did they look like? What did they wear? How has the landscape changed?

Pat Morris has answered these questions admirably in this comprehensive book. She has painstakingly sought out collections of old photographs that have previously been seen by just a few family members. This isn't your run-of-the-mill nostalgia book. Real history has been preserved here, and there should be more books like it before the old photographs fade and crumble.

St. Simons Island has changed dramatically in the past few years. When I first visited here in the early 1950s, there was one traffic light and it was hardly needed save for the weeks between Memorial Day and Labor Day. When I became a permanent resident in the 1970s, Islanders enjoyed the slower pace from September to June. No more. The tempo is busy now all year. All is not lost. An alarming number of mature trees are gone forever, but there are now organizations to preserve our green spaces as well as our heritage.

Old landmarks might have vanished from the landscape but those before us had the forethought to preserve them on film, else we would not have this book.

The book you are holding proceeds chronologically from the earliest Native Americans to the present day. That is the best way to go at the first reading, but you will want to come back to your favorite chapter again and again. As you learn more about the Island, your favorite period may likely change, and that's good. You'll be growing in understanding of this wonderful place.

Old timers here deplore the proliferation of fast-food places; the replacement of charming one-story cottages by three-story palaces blocking views of the sea; and increased traffic, but not all this progress is bad.

The Village area is neater than it once was. Fishermen and strollers enjoy the pier. Much of the beachfront area is open to all, and sunsets are still superb. There are more beautiful residential areas and most people occupying them love the island.

It's certain there are more things to do on the Island than in the good old days. Few are the days when there is not a historical, educational, cultural or just plain fun event to keep all ages entertained. St. Simons Island is blessed with organizations that answer to a great variety of interests, including watching that developers don't go too far.

The good old days may have been great for some, but if you want to see real progress take a look at the bathing suits of yesteryear. Who wants to go to the beach dressed like that!? And what about Fort Frederica? In the old days visitors climbed all over the ruins and even had group photos taken. Today, however, the Fort has been preserved for you and future generations.

In chapter four, you'll learn more about the St. Simons Light than in any other book on the island. You will also see some views of the encampment when troops were stationed here en route to Cuba during the Spanish-American War. We never were invaded by the Spanish, but you can see we were ready for them!

One of the most fun chapters in the book is on tourists to the Golden Isles. The photographs show just how much things have changed—the ladies in their white middy-blouses and hats, the gentlemen in their suits and ties, even the children dressed for a holiday. I'll bet they didn't have "casual Fridays" either. Have we progressed or regressed?

Ms. Morris is splendidly equipped to write this book. Her education and experience have been augmented by her association with the Coastal Georgia Historical Society and the St. Simons Island Lighthouse Museum. In 2000, she was named Executive Director of the society and museum after spending 11 years as the curator of collections. In this publication she has been thoughtful and fun, making this book a welcome addition to the many already written on St. Simons Island.

Edwin H. Ginn
Local Author and Historian

One

A SUMMER RETREAT

NATIVE AMERICANS AND
ST. SIMONS ISLAND

The coast of Georgia was first the domain of the Mocama Indians, previously thought to be the Asao or Guale Indians. In recent research, Dr. John Worth has placed two missions on St. Simons Island. The first, San Buenaventura De Guadalquini, was located at the southern tip of the island. The second mission was thought to be near Cannon's Point on the northern end of the island and called Santa Domingo De Asjo. There were also two villages. San Simon was a Yamasee village and Ocotonico, a pagan Yamasee village, was located south of San Simon and north of the mission San Buenaventura. Tribes most likely spent the spring and summer months on St. Simons.

RESTORED VESSEL. This vessel from Evelyn Mound C illustrates Swift Creek design.

EXCAVATION OF TRENCH ZERO, CHARLES KING MOUND. In 1936, Smithsonian archaeologists were called in when a former burial ground and village was uncovered at the site of what is now called the McKinnon Airport on St. Simons Island. Scientists eventually documented 21,000 artifacts found at this site.

10

UNKNOWN ARCHAEOLOGIST WITH SKELETON. Found during the McKinnon Airport excavation and affectionately called "George" by the locals, the first skeleton uncovered was put on display.

FUNERAL OFFERING. Found at the airport site, this funeral offering included a turtle shell, bear tooth, fish tooth, and pendants.

VIEW TO WEST ACROSS AIRPORT SITE. This photograph shows the thickness of midden, post molds, and midden pits. Excavations in the left middle distance indicate a burial area.

SHELL ORNAMENTS.
This jewelry—including a
mussell shell pendant and
conch shell earrings—was
found at the airport site.

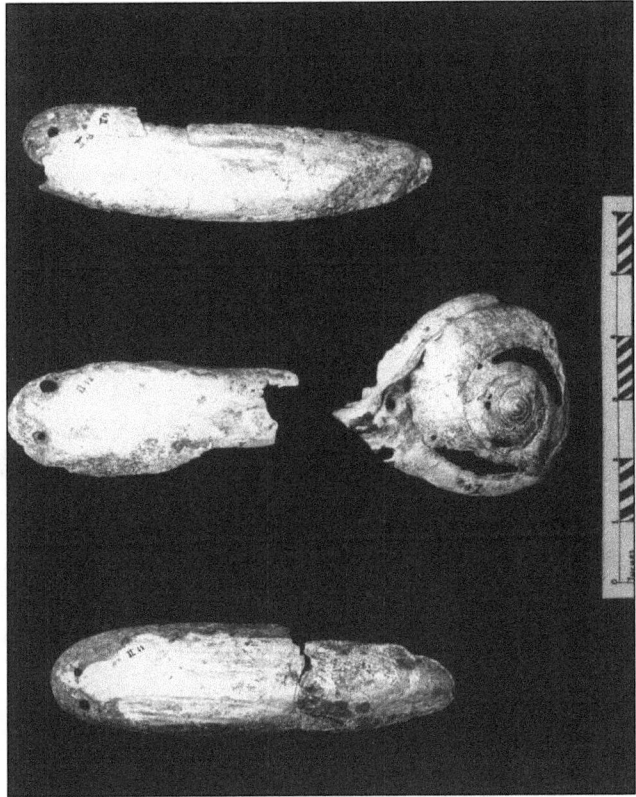

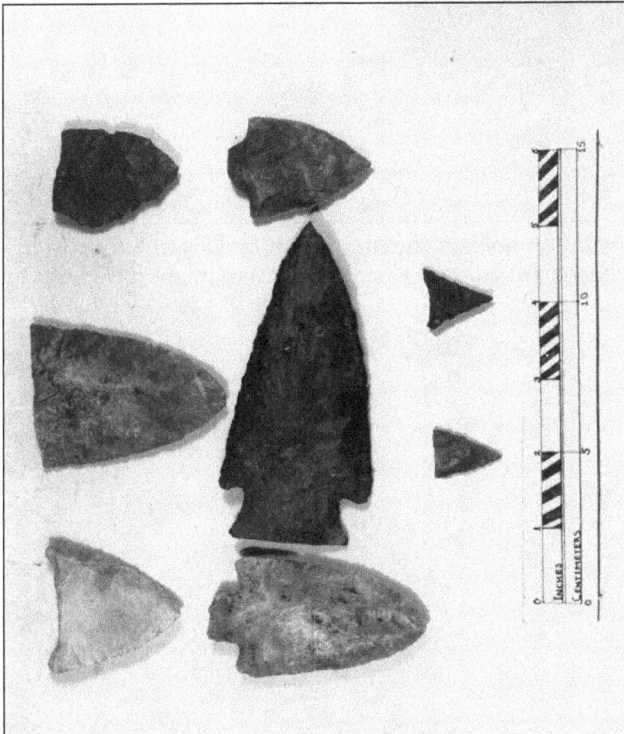

FLINT PROJECTILE POINTS. This
photograph shows the variety
of projectile points found on
St. Simons Island.

McKINNON AIRPORT. This profile shows post molds at the site. A post mold is where a post has rotted away and left a shadow. An archaeologist can tell where a structure might have been by following the shadows.

Two

THE BRITISH AND THE SETTLEMENT OF FORT FREDERICA

With the establishment of the Colony of Carolina in 1670, Spanish dominance in the area was threatened by the English along the Georgia coast. English traders siphoned off Spanish support among the Indians by plying them with cheap goods. Pirates preyed upon the coast and Spanish power and influence soon vanished. By 1686 the Spanish missions were deserted. With the settlement of Savannah in 1733 by Gen. James Oglethorpe, Spain saw England as a larger threat. Oglethorpe then established Fort Frederica to protect Savannah and the Carolinas from Spain. However, with the Battle of Bloody Marsh in 1742, Spain's threat to the Georgia coast was broken and Fort Frederica became a military outpost no longer needed.

OGLETHORPE'S FORT. Strategically placed along the Frederica River, Fort Frederica was a thriving military outpost from 1736 to 1749.

KING'S MAGAZINE. Surrounding the entire settlement of Frederica was a 10-foot earth and timber wall. Within the walls, there were many buildings of brick, wood, and tabby. The final blow to the town of Frederica came in 1758 when it was consumed by fire.

UNKNOWN RESIDENTS. Later called Old Town by local residents, Oglethorpe had named Frederica after Frederick Louis, Prince of Wales, the eldest son of the King and father of George III.

16

RUINS OF OLD FORT. Many locals enjoyed picnicking at the Old fort, *c.* 1898.

DAUGHTERS OF THE AMERICAN REVOLUTION CELEBRATION. In 1903 the Georgia Society of the Colonial Dames of America acquired the remains of the historic fort, and the work of conservation was started. Margaret Davis Cate, local historian, along with Judge and

Mrs. S. Price Gilbert and Alfred W. Jones, formed the Fort Frederica Association in 1941. The Association was instrumental in the formation of Fort Frederica National Monument

KING'S MAGAZINE. By 1783, most of the guns were removed from Fort Frederica and taken to Sunbury, Georgia. This photo is from *c.* 1900.

UNDER THE MIGHTY OAK. In 1945, a donation by the Colonial Dames made establishing Fort Frederica National Monument possible. Today, you can visit the site, which is one of the few archeology parks in the national park system.

SITTING ON RUINS. Visiting the old fort was a favorite pastime of tourists visiting the island in the early 1900s.

POSTCARD OF THE RUINS OF THE OLD FORT. The tabby fort guarded the twisting water approach to the town.

FLYING THE BRITISH FLAG. Only a town for a short time, Fort Frederica was instrumental in securing the area from the Spanish.

RUINS OF FORT FREDERICA. The ruins of Fort Frederica remind us of the struggle for empire two and a half centuries ago.

POSTCARD OF THE BARRACKS. These barracks housed the single soldiers under General Oglethorpe's command.

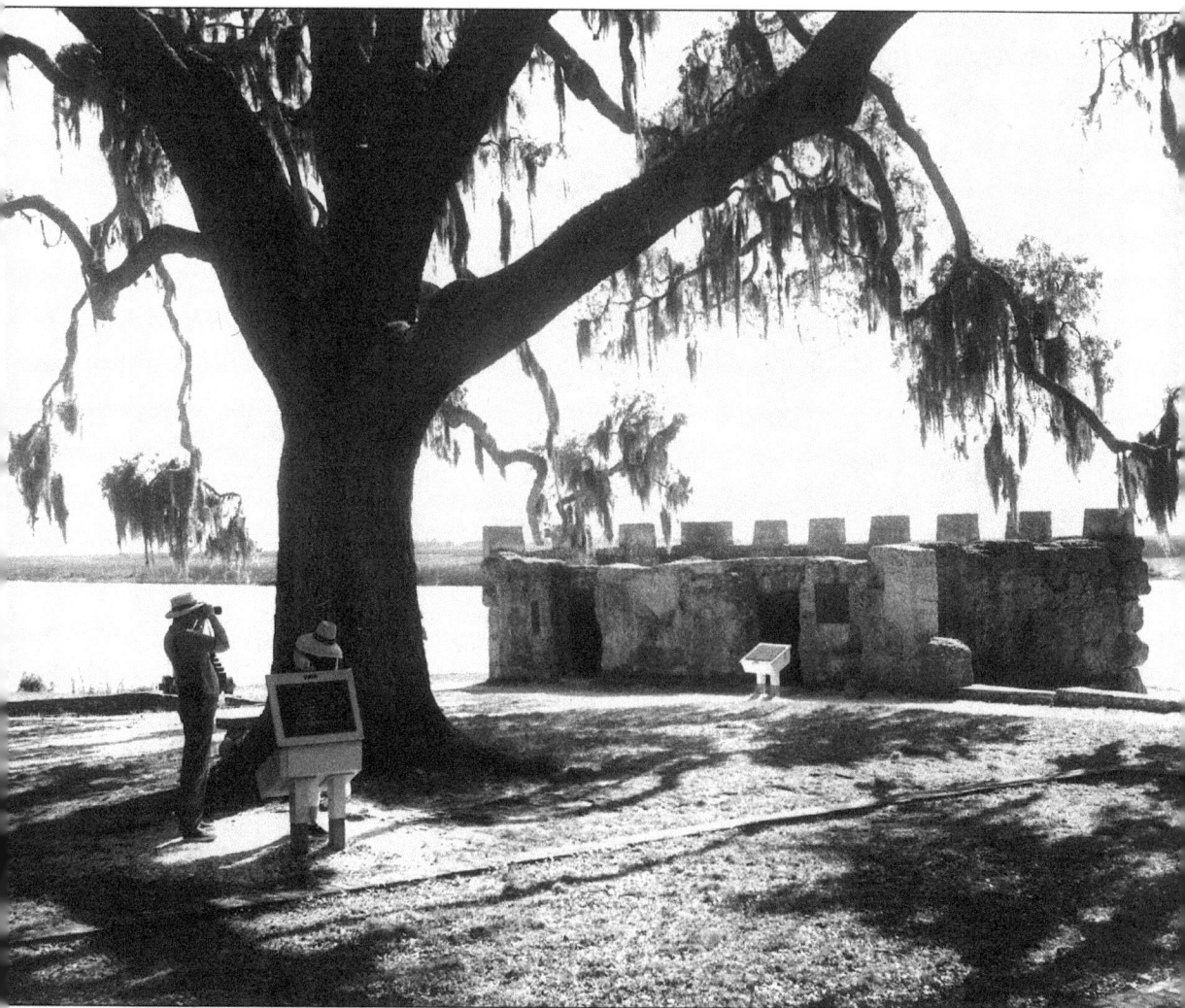

TODAY. Fort Frederica National Monument is an archeological park under the direction of the National Park Service.

Three

St. Simons Island Plantations

During the latter part of the 1700s, several South Carolina planters came to coastal Georgia. They had already prospered, and in turn they created some of the great plantations of the south. The cotton plantations of St. Simons Island were responsible for much of the region's population. Cotton proved to be a lucrative crop and the slave population of Georgia provided the cheap labor. By the early 1800s, a plantation society flourished on St. Simons Island. There following were 14 plantations of note: Cannon's Point, John Couper, owner; Hampton, Maj. Pierce Butler, owner; Pike's, Dr. Thomas Hazzard, owner; West Point, Col. William Hazzard, owner; Lawrence, Capt. John Fraser, owner; Longview, McNish Family, owners; Oatlands, Dr. Grant, owner; Sinclair, Dr. William Fraser, owner; The Village, Capt. Alexander Wylly, owner; Harrington Hall and Mulberry Grove, Capt. Raymond Demere, owner; Hamilton, James Hamilton, owner; Retreat, Maj. William Page, owner; and Kelvin Grove, Thomas Cater, owner. Many planters and their families made St. Simons Island their home year round.

HAMILTON PLANTATION SLAVE CABIN. Charlestown merchant James Hamilton first purchased the property in the late 1800s. His plantation and his shipping docks on the property, still known today as Gascoigne Bluff, became an important part of the local economy.

Brunswick

SAINT SIMONS SOUND

JEKYLL ISLAND

Saint Simons Inlet

SOUTH B

Retreat
(King)

Fort Brown

Hamilton
(Couper)

Lighthouse

(Gould)

Black Ban

Ross
(Ca

Kelvin Grove
(Postell)

Black Ban ed creek

ATLANTIC

Lor

OCEAN

ale   of 2   Miles 3   4

0   160   240   320

als   of   Chains

26

SILK MAP, 1860. This hand-drawn map shows where the island plantations were located. It also represents the local waterways quite well.

SLAVE CHURCH. This church was built of Tabby for the plantation slaves and was thought to be located on St. Simons Island.

HAMILTON PLANTATION SLAVE CABIN. James Hamilton eventually sold his coastal holdings and moved to Philadelphia, leaving the plantation to his namesake, James Hamilton Couper.

Hamilton Plantation Slave Cabin, c. 1900.

KELVIN GROVE PLANTATION. Bought in the 1790s, upon Thomas Cater's death this plantation became the property of his son Benjamin Franklin Cater. William Page oversaw the management of the plantation until Benjamin became of legal age. Cater's daughter married James Postell of South Carolina and they made their home at Kelvin Grove. The Postells were one of the few families to return to the island after the Civil War. (From a painting by Mildred Huie.)

BLACK BANKS PLANTATION. In the early 1800s, James Gould purchased the land for his eldest son, James, who had recently graduated from Yale University and married a girl from New England. His wife never adjusted to island living and before moving north, James sold Black Banks to his younger brother, Horace.

Tabby Huts in Slave Quarters,
West Point Plantation.
ST. SIMONS ISLAND, Ga.

RUINS OF WEST POINT PLANTATION SLAVE QUARTERS. Owned originally by Col. William Hazzard, West Point was just south of his brother, Dr. Thomas Hazzard's plantation of Pike Bluff. The two brothers were well-known in the community. Colonel Hazzard wrote an early history of Glynn County while his brother, Thomas, became infamous in dispute over boundaries with John Wylly of the Village. Dr. Hazzard shot Wylly and was tried for aggravated manslaughter but was found innocent.

RUINS AT HAMPTON PLANTATION. At the end of the 18th century, Maj. Pierce Butler, South Carolina's delegate to the new Congress, purchased the land at the north end of St. Simons Island. First used by Oglethorpe as an outpost against a surprise attack by the Spanish, Hampton Point is probably best known because of Fanny Kemble Butler's journal entries. In a 1839 visit, Kemble wrote of the deterioration of this once-elegant plantation.

RUINS AT HAMPTON PLANTATION.

CANNON'S POINT PLANTATION. Built in 1804, John Couper had an interest in horticulture and collected plants from around the world. A successful merchant in Sunbury, Georgia, Couper purchased land on St. Simons in partnership with James Hamilton and moved to the island with his bride, Rebecca. (From a painting by John Lord Couper, grandson of John and Rebecca Couper.)

MR. AND MRS. WILLIAM AUDLEY COUPER, C. 1887. William's father was John Couper, whose plantation prospered in the early 1800s. Like many plantation owners, John Couper traveled extensively, but unlike many other plantation owners, the Coupers made their home on St. Simons. In the early 1840s, William became manager of Hamilton Plantation. He married Hannah Page King of Retreat Plantation.

WILLIAM AUDLEY COUPER AND SONS, C. 1887. "I know your sense of having done your duty will be the richest satisfaction you can enjoy," James Hamilton Couper once wrote to his sister, Anne. But this quote can be applied to all the Couper children as they fulfilled their duty of carrying on the legacy.

RUINS OF CANNON'S POINT PLANTATION, C. 1970. Moving to Cannon's Point in 1794, the Coupers set about to create a large plantation home. It was finally completed in 1804.

Maj. William Page built the Retreat Plantation into one of the wealthiest in the South. Spalding was the first to receive a seed of cotton known as Anguilla cotton. Today, it is known as Sea Island cotton.

ANNA MATILDA. As her father's interests grew, Major Paige was frequently away from home. His daughter Anna Matilda proved to have the skills required for management of a busy plantation.

THOMAS BUTLER KING. In 1824, Anna married Thomas Butler King, one of the wealthiest planters in Georgia. Like his father-in-law, King became active in politics and spent much of his time away from home. Anna continued to run the plantation as a profitable business.

Kings Road   "The Retreat"
St Simons Island Ga   1887

RETREAT PLANTATION. In 1887, the road leading to the main house was overgrown.

RETREAT PLANTATION HOUSE. Built as temporary, the Retreat Plantation House was never replaced. Instead, additions were simply added when needed. The house is no longer standing,

but the Retreat barn is now part of the Sea Island Golf Club.

RUINS OF THE RETREAT SLAVE HOSPITAL. Slaves at Retreat were treated better than most. William Page built the hospital that his daughter Anna Matilda staffed in order to meet the health needs of the plantation slaves.

RUINS OF THE RETREAT SLAVE HOSPITAL. Page's Plantation prospered and his slaves were treated better than most.

THE KING'S ROAD. Located today on the grounds of the Sea Island golf course, the Avenue of Oaks can still be seen.

KING FAMILY PORTRAIT. Anna Matilda died in 1859 and the Civil War brought an end to Retreat Plantation. The land remained with the King family, however, until 1926 when it was sold to the Sea Island Company. This photo was taken at the turn of the century.

NEPTUNE SMALL. Neptune Small was born a slave and owned by the King family of Retreat Plantation. During the Civil War he accompanied Capt. Lord King as his cook and companion until the time of the Captain's death at Fredericksburg, Virginia. When Captain Lord failed to returned after the battle, Small searched the battlefield until he found his dead master and carried the body back to Savannah. He then returned to the war with the King's youngest son, Cuyler, who returned home unharmed.

SMALL AND THE KING BOYS. After the war, Small returned to Retreat Plantation. He was a special friend to the King boys and gained a position of respect in the family. From left to right are John Floyd King, Capt. Charles Spalding Wylly, Jacob Dart, and M.J. Colson. Neptune Small is standing.

43

PIER LOOKING TOWARD LIGHTHOUSE. The St. Simons Lighthouse has been an important part of the island community for many years, c. 1910.

Four

AIDS TO NAVIGATION

THE ST. SIMONS ISLAND
LIGHT STATION

As the plantations prospered, shipping became an important part of plantation life on St. Simons Island. In 1804, John Couper of Cannon's Point Plantation deeded four acres of his land at the south end of the island—known as Couper's Point—to the federal government for the construction of a lighthouse. James Gould of Massachusetts was hired to build the lighthouse and became the first keeper. The 75-foot tower was constructed of tabby, a material mixed from oyster shells, sand, water, and lime. The island prospered until the War Between the States. The blockade of federal ships and the subsequent invasion of Georgia by Northern troops forced the Confederates to evacuate St. Simons Island. But before they left in 1862, they destroyed the lighthouse to insure Union shipping would not use it as a navigational aid.

A second boom period came many years after the war when lumber mills were established on the island. The second lighthouse was built in 1872 by Georgian architect Charles Cluskey. The 104-foot tower had 129 cast iron steps and an adjacent keeper's house. Cluskey and some of his crew never saw the fruition of their efforts. They died of malaria in 1871 before the lighthouse was completed.

GOULD'S LIGHTHOUSE. The first lighthouse was lit in 1811. The 75-foot tower was an octagonal pyramid with a 10-foot iron lantern equipped with oil lamps suspended by chains.

45

PORTRAIT OF FIRST LIGHTHOUSE KEEPER. James Gould held the position of keeper until his retirement in 1837 at an annual salary of $400. He was also a successful planter and owned St.Clair/Black Banks. His descendants still reside on St. Simons Island.

RUINS OF FIRST LIGHTHOUSE. The ruins of the first lighthouse were partially excavated by archaeologists in August 1974.

St. Simons Island Lighthouse, 1872. The building of the second lighthouse on St. Simons began in 1867. Charles Cluskey was one of the more important architects of his time, designing Greek Revival buildings throughout Georgia between 1830 and 1846.

47

CLUSKEY CREW. Cluskey and a number of his crew died of malaria in 1871 and the project had to be completed by his overseer. Official records of the lighthouse keeper stated in 1874,: "This station is very unhealthy, and it is attributed to the stagnant water in several ponds in the vicinity."

U. S. Light House, St. Simon Island, Ga.
Pub. by C. M. Tilton, Brunswick, Ga.

LIGHTHOUSE AT THE TURN OF THE CENTURY. The lighthouse grounds have always been a well-cared-for station.

LIGHTHOUSE KEEPER. This is an unidentified assistant lighthouse keeper after a successful hunting trip.

UNIDENTIFIED GENTLEMEN, EARLY 1900s. Visitors to the island enjoyed stopping in to visit the lighthouse keeper.

ST. SIMONS RANGE FRONT BEACON, C. 1896. Range beacons are defined as two lights, located a distance apart, visible from one direction only. When one light is visible directly above the other, you can navigate the marked channel safely. Today the St. Simons Light continues to use

range beacons, but a shot-gun approach is taken. By lining up the lighthouse in the center of the two range beacons, one can pass the channel safely.

LIGHTHOUSE IN 1914.

ON THE STEPS, 1922. C.O. Svendsen Jr. and his sister Happy posed for the traditional shot on the lighthouse steps. C.O. doesn't look too happy.

LIGHTHOUSE KEEPER. C.O. Svendson was keeper of the St. Simons Light from 1907 through 1936.

SVENDSON FAMILY. The Svendson family enjoyed St. Simons Island. Carl Jr. often spoke of the many happy days he spent fishing and exploring the island.

JINX, THE SVENDSEN DOG. Family members said that Jinx was able to hear the footsteps of the ghost of a former keeper and it scared him.

RENOVATIONS. Around 1910, the dwelling was altered into two apartments by removing the indoor central staircase and adding an exterior staircase, stoop, and door.

LIGHTHOUSE IN 1919. The keeper was not only responsible for the light but the grounds as well. Erosion has taken away much of the land by the lighthouse.

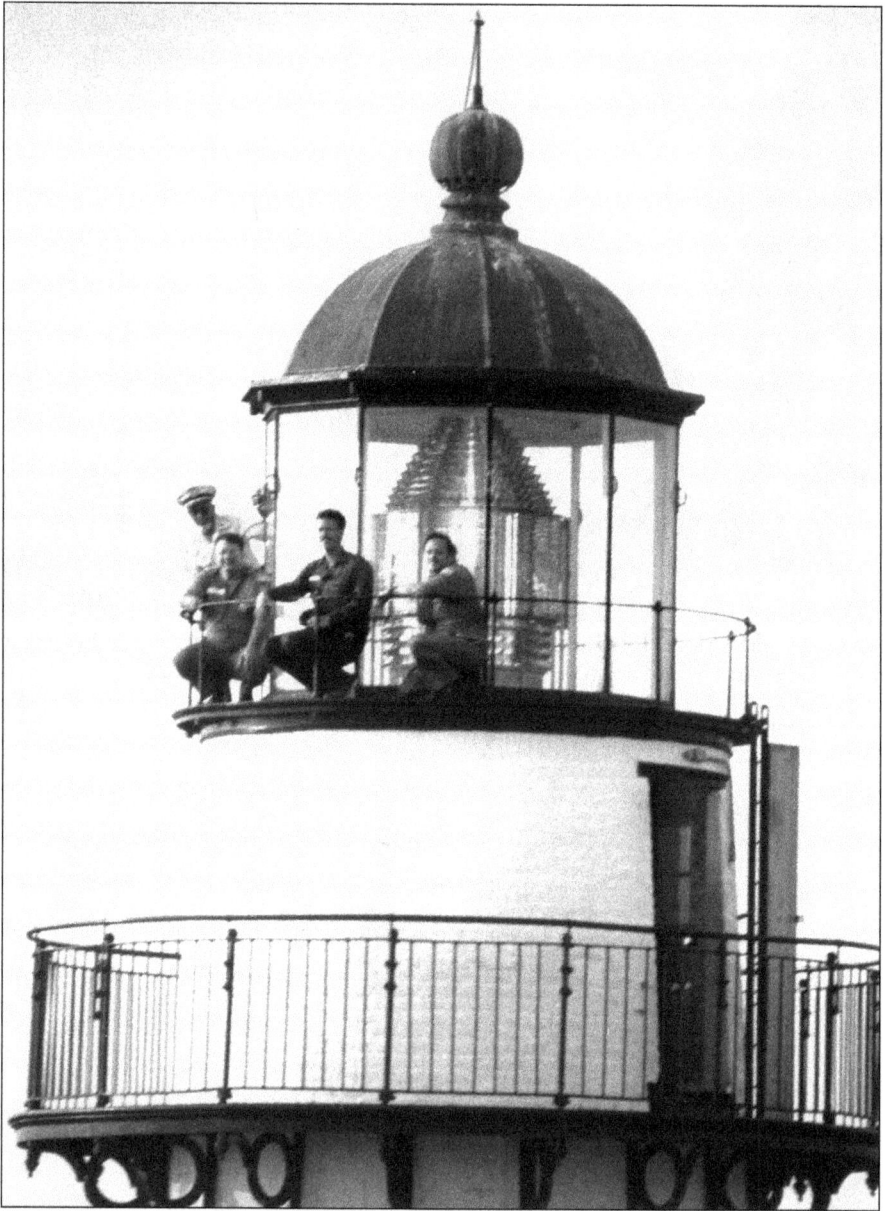

CARETAKERS. The Coast Guard Auxiliary continues to care for the Fresnel Lens. From left to right are Bernie Long, Bob West, Jeff Cole, and Dave Melvin.

FAR-REACHING LIGHT. The third-order Fresnel lens projects 23 miles out to sea.

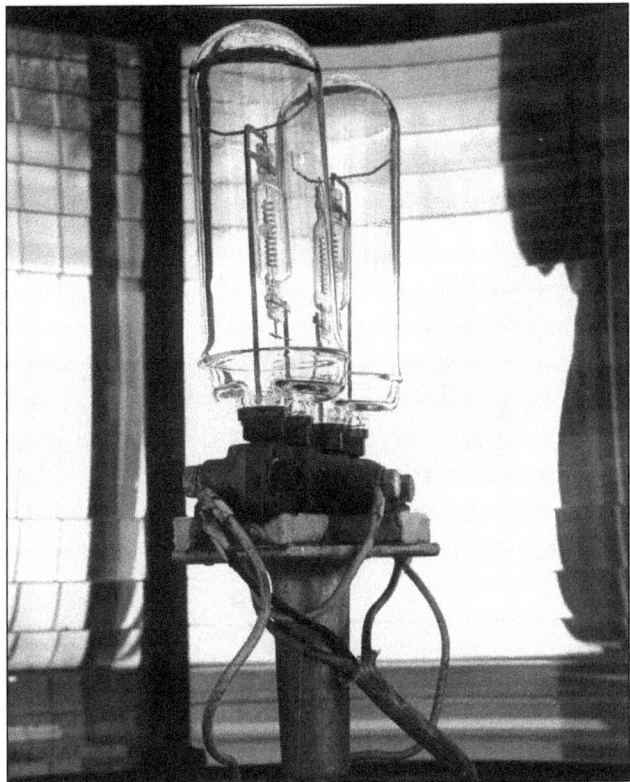

MODERNIZATION. Electrified in 1934, the lighthouse is fully automated and produces one beam per minute.

57

COAST GUARD STATION. In 1936, a Coast Guard Station was built on East Beach for search and rescue. The lighthouse was placed under Coast Guard jurisdiction in 1939.

BEACH. Much of the beach in front of the lighthouse was lost during Hurricane Dora in 1963.

58

CHRISTMAS SNOW. In 1989, an unusual white Christmas covered the lighthouse in snow.

CHANGES. Once a lonely station, the lighthouse is now surrounded by development, making it a focal point for many activities on St. Simons.

STILL GOING. The light still shines brightly out to sea.

LIGHTHOUSE MUSEUM. Today, the lighthouse is owned and operated by the Coastal Georgia Historical Society as a museum. Visitors can still climb the 129 steps to the top.

Five

THE LUMBER MILLS

At the end of the Civil War, the island's recovery hinged on the need around the world for lumber. Norman W. Dodge purchased Hamilton Plantation and many came to work the mills and docks at Gascoigne Bluff. The Dodge-Meigs Company acquired 300,000 acres in Georgia. Timber was cut, then floated down the Satilla and Althamaha Rivers to the lumber mills at the Bluff. "The Mills" became a community where people worked and lived, remaining active until the lumber supply declined in the early 1900s. During this time, Anson Green Phelps Dodge Jr. came to St. Simons Island and re-established Christ Church. His second wife later began a home for orphan boys called "The Dodge Home."

TAYLOR CREEK CYPRESS MILLS, C. 1890.

CHRIST CHURCH.
First established by the early settlers after the Revolutionary War, the church was incorporated in 1808. The first church was erected in 1820.

CHRIST CHURCH. As a memorial to his first wife, who died on their honeymoon, the Rev. Anson Green Phelps Dodge Jr. rebuilt Christ Church.

ANSON DODGE AND HIS FIRST WIFE ELLEN. On a wedding trip, the Dodges visited St. Simons and became interested in the old Christ Church. When Ellen died on a trip around the world, Anson built the church in her memory.

SUNDAY SCHOOL CLASS UNDER THE OAKS, 1917. Christ Church Sunday School classes still meet under the oaks today.

CHRIST CHURCH TODAY. The church is cruciform in design with memorials, commemorating

the life of Christ and the early history of the church on St. Simons.

WORKERS IN JEWTOWN. Sig and Robert Levison, prominent Brunswick citizens, built a store about a mile from the mills at Gascoigne Bluff. When a few houses sprung up around the store, the neighborhood was given the name of Jewtown, in honor of its founders.

MR. EUGENE W. LEWIS IN LUMBER OFFICE. Ownership of the mills changed a number of times. With the decline of the mills, the mill property at Gascoigne Bluff remained vacant until 1927 when it was purchased by Howard Coffin.

GASCOIGNE BLUFF. Joseph Hilton and Norman Dodge joined to form the Hilton-DodgeCompany that included six mills at Darien and one on the Satilla River in addition to the mill at Gascoigne Bluff. It was believed that these mills could cut over a million feet of lumber a year.

WRIGHT AND GOWEN GENERAL STORE AND POST OFFICE. The "Mills" was a community of gingerbread trim, gardens, and walkways. A church, schoolhouse, and general store (converted from the old Hamilton Plantation barn) helped to make the mill settlement a pleasant place to live at the turn of the century.

TAYLOR COOK CYPRESS MILL. This was part of the Mill Village around 1890 and was Phil Hopkins House.

TAYLOR COOK CYPRESS MILLS. The mills closed in 1905.

ANNA GOULD DODGE. Daughter of the Gould family of Black Banks Plantation, Anna was the second wife of Reverend Dodge. When Dodge died as a young man, Anna supervised the Anson Dodge Home for Boys, a memorial to their young son who was killed in a carriage accident when only three years old.

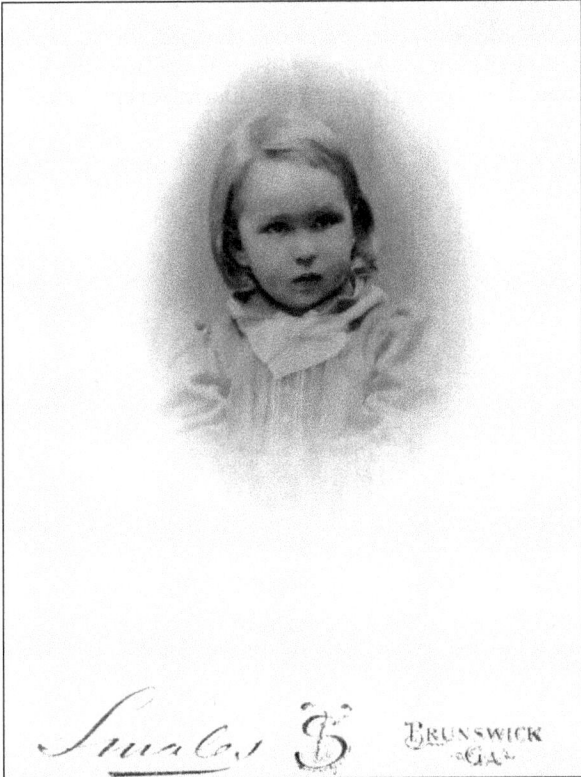

ANSON DODGE JR. When little more than a baby, the son of Anson and Anna Dodge was fatally injured in a horse-drawn carriage accident.

Dodge Home, Early 1900s. The Dodge Home for Boys operated until the mid-1950s. It provided an island home for many young men. The site of the original building was included in Fort Frederica National Monument.

FIRST DODGE HOME. Anna Gould managed the home until her death in 1927.

UNDER THE OAKS. Boys from Dodge Home are seen here enjoying the outdoors.

INSIDE THE DODGE HOME. A family setting was provided for many boys.

TYPICAL SCHOOL ROOM. Schooling was provided for many boys who would not have had the opportunity to attend otherwise.

Six

THE MILITARY COMES TO ST. SIMONS

First settled as a military outpost, St. Simons is no stranger to the military. St. Simons has a long history of military occupation beginning in Oglethorpe's time and ending with World War II. During the Spanish-American War, the island once again protected the shores from Spanish attack. As a military training area and Naval airfield during World War II, the island and its residents once again help to protect the shores and the port of Brunswick from enemy attack.

SPANISH-AMERICAN WAR. Camp Barker, located near the lighthouse, saw troops protecting the coastline during the Spanish-American War.

SPANISH-AMERICAN WAR. This is an 1898 encampment of the North Carolina Regiment near the lighthouse.

NEAR LIGHTHOUSE. Pictured above is a signal station by the lighthouse during the Spanish-American War.

LEISURE TIME FOR SOLDIERS DURING SPANISH-AMERICAN WAR. This is the reading and pool room for the eighth infantry.

CANNON ALONG THE COAST. Although the cannons were never fired against the enemy, they were probably used for training.

STRACHAN COTTAGE. A cannon was placed in front of the Strachan Cottage during the Spanish-American War, 1900. (From the collection of Diane Jackson.)

MAIN ENTRANCE. World War II saw military activity once again on St. Simons Island. This is the main entrance to the United States Naval Air Station located on the island between 1942 and 1945.

AERIAL VIEW OF ST. SIMONS ISLAND ON NOVEMBER 25, 1945. Note that someone has written "help" in the sand.

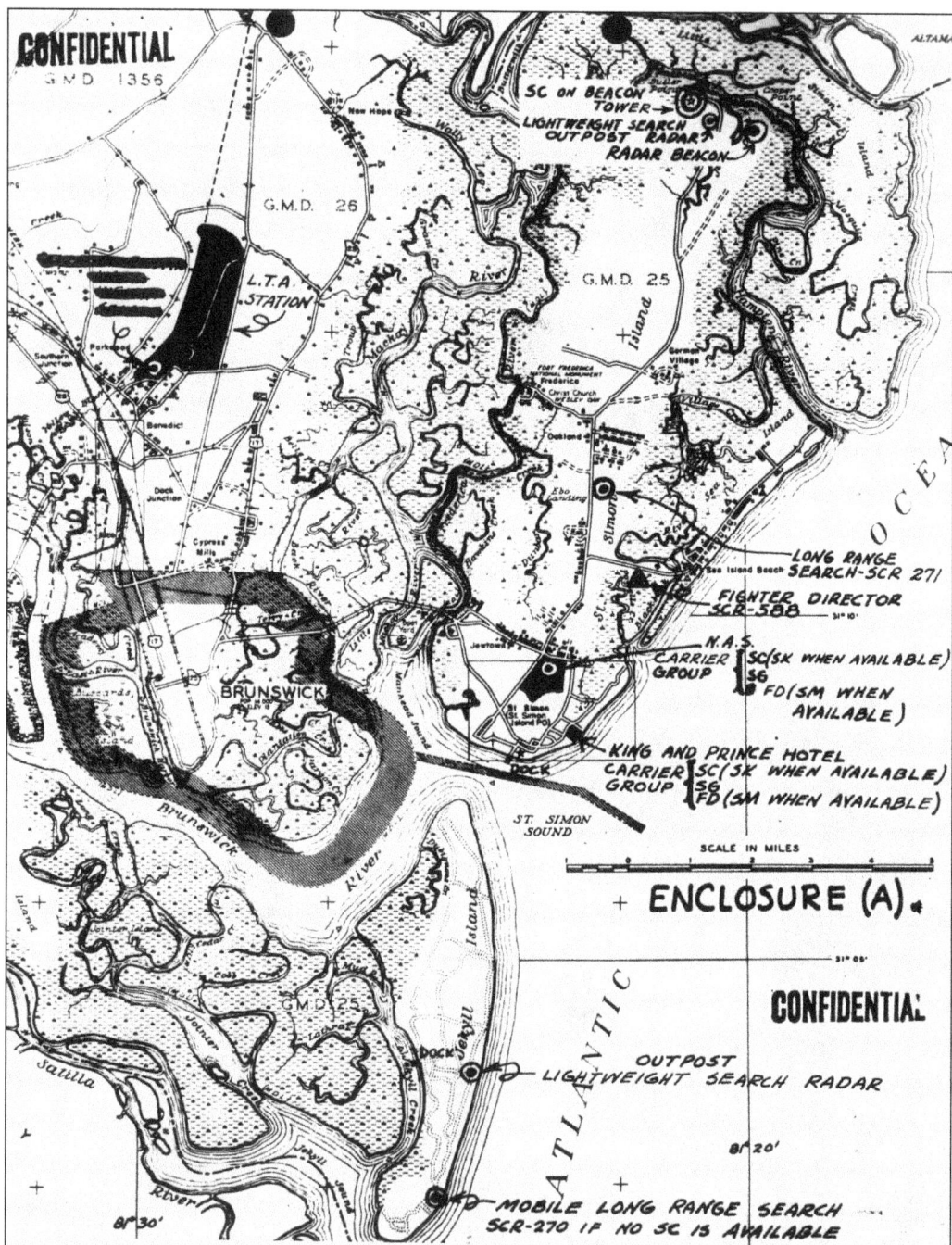

MAP RELEASED AFTER THE WAR. This map shows the extent of United States Naval involvement on St. Simons Island as well as surrounding areas.

KING & PRINCE HOTEL. Used as living quarters for Naval personnel, the King & Prince Hotel was also used as a radar training school.

PROTECTIVE HOTEL. Outfitted for war, the hotel helped to limit German U-Boat activity along the coast.

KING & PRINCE DOCK. This view was taken after a storm in 1948.

AERIAL VIEW OF THE KING & PRINCE HOTEL.

RADAR ROOM. Men were trained on the latest radar technology at the King & Prince.

SPOTTED. Reconnaissance activity around the island captured a patrol close to the island.

ST. SIMONS ISLAND COASTLINE, C. 1945. The Georgia coast provided a good opportunity for flight reconnaissance training.

U-BOAT ACTIVITY. With the increased shipping traffic off the coast of St. Simons Island, German U-Boats became a problem. In April of 1942, the *Esso Baton Rouge* and the *SS Oklahoma* were attacked.

DRY DOCK. This is a hull of a ship pulling into dry dock after being hit with a torpedo from a German U-Boat off the coast of St. Simons.

SALVAGE OPERATIONS. Twenty-two men lost their lives during the German U-Boat attack on the SS *Oklahoma* and *Esso Baton Rouge*, and the war came home to island residents.

LIBERTY SHIP. A damaged Liberty ship is seen in dry dock, *c.* 1942.

SALVAGE OPERATIONS.

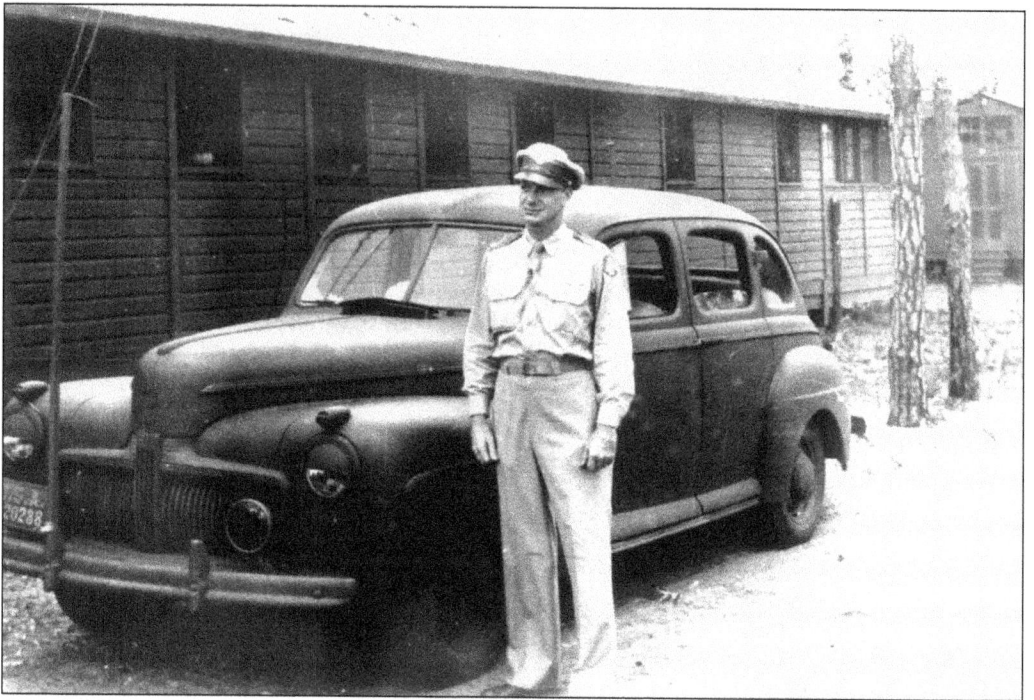

CAPTAIN FLINT AT LIVING QUARTERS. In addition to the radar training school at the King & Prince, the Malcolm McKinnon airfield became a home base for a carrier group of torpedo bombers.

AERIAL VIEW OF MCKINNON AIRFIELD. The airport was first opened in 1938. Eastern Airlines later opened a terminal on St. Simons Island under Eastern president Eddie Rickenbacker.

PREPARING FOR A MISSION, C. 1942. The Civil Air Patrol also helped to patrol the water around St. Simons.

A CREW AT MCKINNON AIR FIELD. McKinnon airport was much improved by the Navy.

McKinnon Airfield. Patrols of torpedo planes flew over St. Simons during the war.

Crew at United States Naval Air Station, St. Simons Island. Many servicemen who were trained on St. Simons returned to make it their home after the war.

LIVING QUARTERS. Not all living quarters were in the comfort of the local hotels. Many soldiers lived in tents.

LIVING QUARTERS ON ST. SIMONS ISLAND. While St. Simons' climate is moderate, soldiers had to deal with humidity and insects.

NAVAL OFFICER. Captain Flint inspects camp.

MISSION COMPLETED. This aircraft is just in from a mission. Note the bomb under the aircraft.

OFFICERS AT MCKINNON AIR FIELD. Built by Glynn County in 1938, Malcolm McKinnon Airport was taken over by the Navy at the beginning of World War II. A much improved civilian airport was opened after the war. It is still an active airport today.

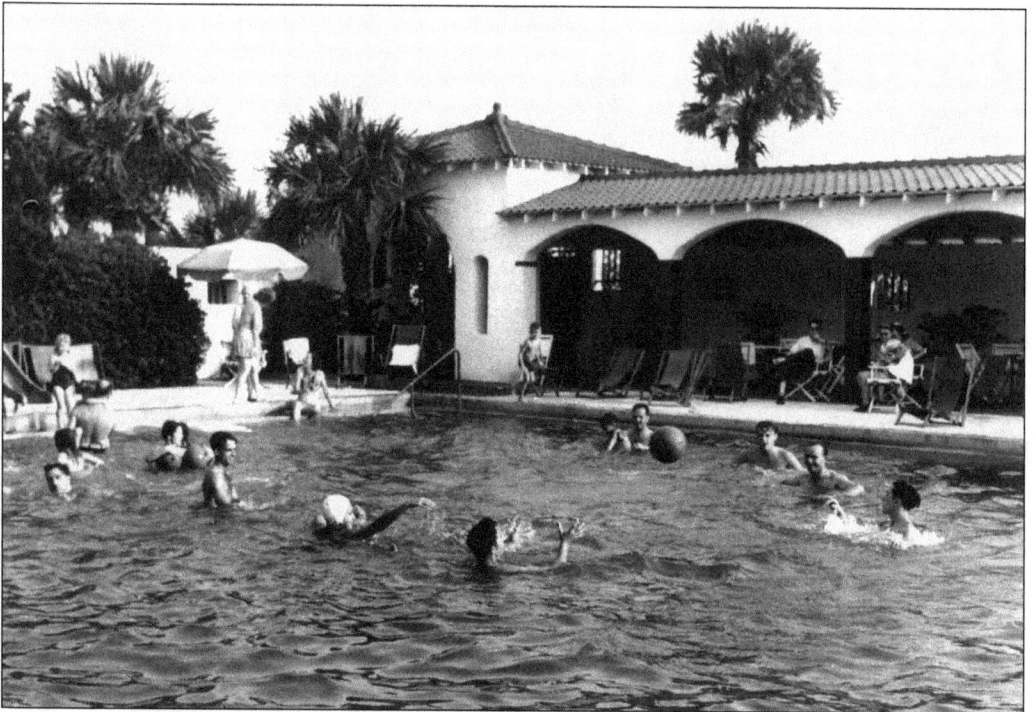

THE CLOISTER HOTEL. Island duty was not all work and no play. The Cloister opened its door to the servicemen for a variety of activities. Here servicemen and their families enjoy a swim in the hotel pool.

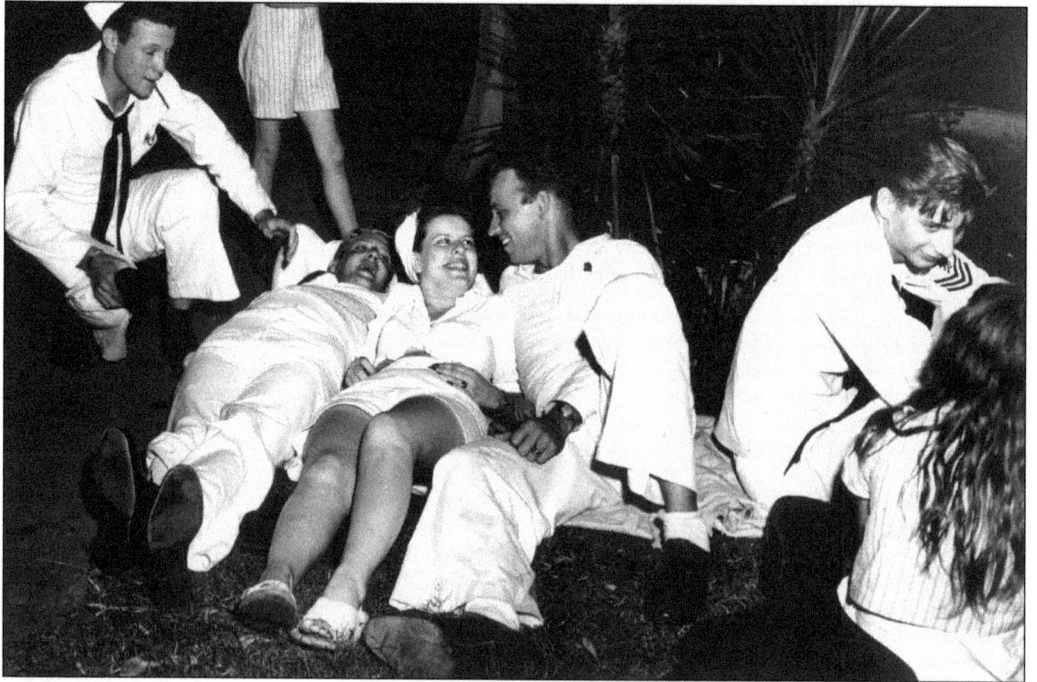

UNDER THE OAKS. A picnic under the oaks was a good way for servicemen to relax and meet some of the local ladies.

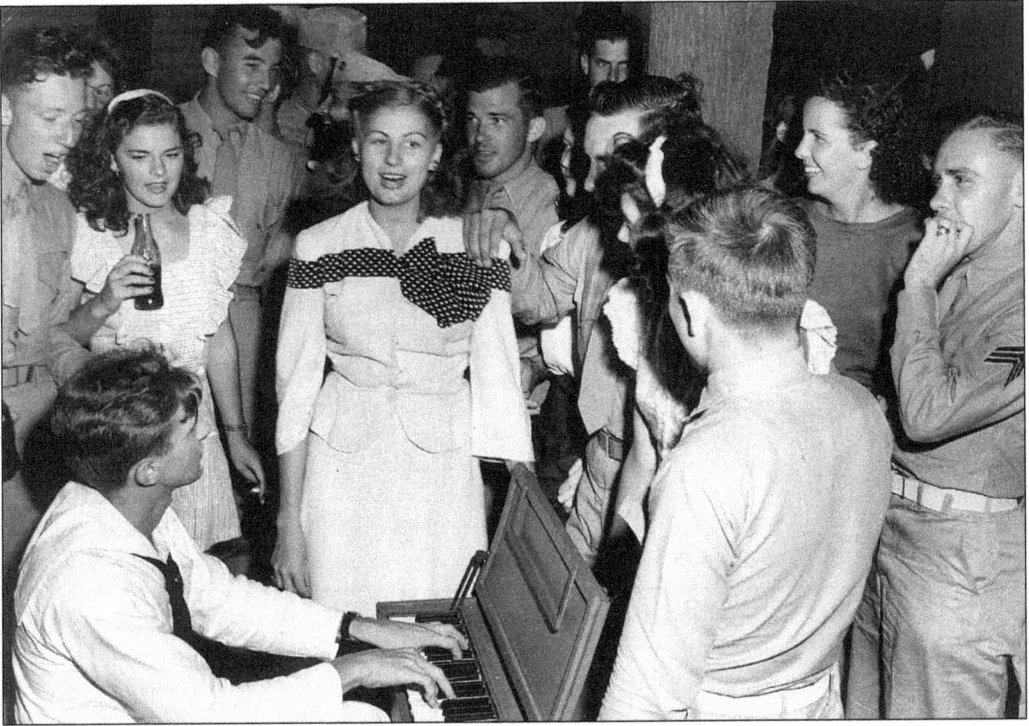

SING-ALONG WITH MITCH. A good time was had by all as servicemen enjoy a few hours off.

AND A ONE-TWO-THREE. Dancing was another favorite way to pass the evenings.

NIGHT ON THE TOWN. Chief Boggs enjoys a night out with Iccleberg, Siegle, White, Hopkins, Brown, and Gierson.

THE LOO. A "touch of home" spruces up military quarters.

Seven

TOURISM

NEW GROWTH FOR THE ISLAND

By the 1880s tourism was in full swing on St. Simons Island. The mild climate and beaches drew visitors to the island as a year-round resort. With the opening of the mills came regular steamship service between St. Simons and the mainland. The island not only became a summer retreat for those in Brunswick but also for families from Waycross and Baxley, Georgia. The Brunswick-St. Simons Highway, known today as the Torras Causeway, was opened in 1924. This was a milestone in the development of the resorts on the island.

ST. SIMONS PIER. With the advent of steam travel, tourists flocked to the island beginning in the 1870s.

TILTON'S WATER SLIDE. The beaches of St. Simons proved to be a draw for tourists. The pier area continues as a favorite place to enjoy the beach, although the water slide is no longer there.

HOTEL BELLEVUE. The former Hotel Bellevue became the St. Simons Hotel *c.* 1916.

ST. SIMONS HOTEL. The hotel was a center of activity with rooms above, and shops and a post office below.

St. Simons Pier, 1920s. The paddlewheel *City of Brunswick* made a daily run to deliver visitors to the island.

Pier Hotel. Northeast of the pier and lighthouse was Tilton's Pier Hotel.

CHAPMAN'S WHARF C. 1890.

SEA GATE. The pier was constructed in 1887 at the south end of the island. Regular passenger service was supplied from the mainland by the *Sea Gate*, *Emmeline*, *Hessie*, *Atlantic*, *Attaquin*, and the *City of Brunswick*

EMMELINE. This ferry carried vacationers to their island retreat on St. Simons.

DORY ON PILOT BOAT GRACEY. Pilot boats are still used today to help navigate St. Simons Sound.

HORSE AND BUGGY. Visitors to the island reached the hotels in a number of ways, c. 1911.

MULE-DRAWN TROLLEY. Eventually, rails were laid along Railroad Avenue, now known as Beachview.

TROLLEY IN THE VILLAGE, 1900. A trolley met visitors at the pier and transported them to the various hotels.

THE LIMITED ALONG RAILROAD AVENUE.

The Jeep Train, St. Simons Island, Ga.

K7993

JEEP TRAIN. The "Jeep Train" was formerly known as the "Mule Train."

HOTEL ST. SIMONS, 1888. Built by the Brunswick Company, the hotel accommodated 300 summer visitors. The hotel burned in 1898.

NEW ST. SIMONS HOTEL, 1911. The New St. Simons Hotel was built in 1910 by Burns-Gibson of Waycross on the site of the Hotel St. Simons.

THE ARNOLD HOUSE. Rates to stay at the Arnold House were $2 to $3 per day and $11 to $13 per week.

THE SHIP HOUSE. With an unusual design, their motto was "Nothing like it in the World."

MORNING CATCH. Fishing and crabbing were also popular pastimes on the island.

ST. SIMONS ISLAND HUNTING CLUB. This is possibly a hunting camp at the north end of the island in the early 1900s. (Photo courtesy of Diane Jackson collection.)

TENTS AT HUNTING CLUB, EARLY 1900S. Game included birds, deer, and wild boar. (Photo courtesy of Diane Jackson collection.)

HUNTING CLUB. Cooks cleaned and prepared game at the camp. (Photo courtesy of Diane Jackson collection.)

ON THE BEACH, ST. SIMONS ISLAND, GA.

THE BEACH. This postcard shows summer visitors enjoying the sun and surf.

GENTLEMEN UNDER THE OAKS. A picnic under the live oaks was a favorite summer pastime at the turn of the century.

108

MRS. BROWN'S DRY GOODS STORE, 1898. Located in the Village, Mrs. Brown supplied the visitor and local alike with necessary notions.

ST. SIMONS ISLAND FROM A PAINTING. From 1892 to 1907, Joseph Champagne was lighthouse keeper. Here he shows his talent as an artist.

OFFICIAL PROGRAM

—OF—

OPENING EXERCISES

—AND—

HISTORICAL PAGEANT

PRESENTED IN CONNECTION
WITH THE OPENING OF THE

BRUNSWICK-ST. SIMONS
HIGHWAY

JULY 11TH, 1924

SPONSORED BY THE
WOMAN'S CLUB OF BRUNSWICK

CAUSEWAY PROGRAM, 1924. On July 11, 1924, Brunswick-St. Simons Highway was opened, changing the island forever.

BUILDING THE CAUSEWAY. As a series of roads and bridges, the causeway made it possible for many to visit St. Simons and its beaches.

FERNANDO TORRAS. Torras was the engineer in charge of the project and the causeway was later renamed for him.

OPENING CEREMONY FOR THE CAUSEWAY. Speeches by state and local dignitaries, a historical pageant, and a parade with brightly decorated automobiles added to the festivities of the day that was to change the direction of St. Simons' future.

CHRISTENING THE BRIDGE. The causeway bridge was christened by Katherine McKinnon as her father Mayor McKinnon, Governor Walker, and others look on.

MACKAYS RIVER TRESTLE   BRUNSWICK–ST. SIMON'S HIGHWAY, GEORGIA

MACKAY'S RIVER BRIDGE. The causeway brought the first day trippers to the island.

Paul Redfern, On the Right. Owner of a garage at the corner of Mallory and Beachview, Paul Redfern was also a local pilot.

Preparing for His Trip, 1927. Redfern spent much of his time flying over marshes and woods.

Jack— I do have a picture in front
of Redfern's airplane, made August
1927. I wore white shirt and white
short trousers. Was standing with left
hand on hip and holding little girls
hand— Her name was Mary Hagen
child of Mr-Mrs Frank Hagen.
    I was 6 and she 4. I suffered
a near heat or sun stroke that day
and was sick for some time after—
    How's your golf?
                    Hugh B—

PAUL REDFERN, LOCAL HERO. Local children joined in the excitement of the Redfern flight. This photograph was taken right before the flight in August 1927.

TAKING OFF FROM THE BEACH. After much fanfare, Redfern left on a long-distance flight to Brazil. His plane was later found in the Amazon jungle.

WAYCROSS COLONY. This is a view from the top of St. Simons Island Lighthouse. Beginning in the 1890s, the Waycross Colony became home to many over the summer months.

Typical Residence at the Turn of the Century. A group of simply built summer cottages, the Waycross Colony was wiped out by the storm of 1898. They were later rebuilt and burned in 1935.

On the Porch, c. 1900. The gentlemen usually stayed on the mainland during the weekend and came to the island to join family on the weekend. (Photo courtesy of the Diane Jackson collection.)

WAYCROSS COLONY. The cottages were of crude design; they also lacked electric lights and plumbing.

ON THE BEACH, 1900. Playing in the surf was a favorite pastime of those who spent the summer on the island, c. 1900. (Photo courtesy of the Diane Jackson collection.)

118

TYPICAL STREET IN THE WAYCROSS
COLONY. Many friends were made
over the course of a summer.

A LAZY AFTERNOON. As a summer retreat
from the heat of the mainland, many came
every summer. There was always a time to
relax and enjoy the day.

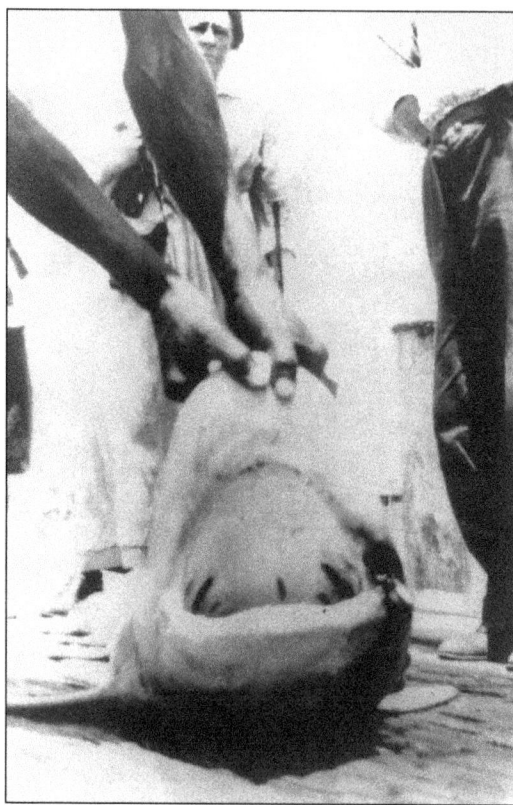

SHARK AT ST. SIMONS ISLAND PIER, c. 1920. Shark fishing is still a popular pastime for the pier.

PRIVATE COTTAGES AND BEACH, ST. SIMONS ISLAND, BRUNSWICK, GA.

VIEW OF ST. SIMONS ISLAND BEACH. Private homes and cottages continued to pop up along the beaches of St. Simons.

GLYNN HAVEN, C. 1950. While many spent time at the beach, others enjoyed the freshwater lakes on the island.

THE CASINO. Built to replace the St. Simons Hotel, the first casino had a pier that extended to the sound.

CASINO, EARLY 1920S. A favorite meeting place for locals, the casino was a place to enjoy dancing and other activities, although it was never a gambling establishment.

CASINO FIRE, 1933. Built entirely of wood, it did not take long for the casino to burn.

Casino Swimming Pool, St. Simon Island, Ga.

NEW CASINO, 1951. Built as a recreation center for the island and designed by Cormack McGarvey, the New Casino also had a swimming pool still used today.

POPULAR PLACE. The St. Simons pier continues still as a gathering place for tourists and locals alike.

BOY SCOUTS. In the early 1930s, the Boys Scouts of America enjoyed Camp Fendig on St. Simons Island.

CARNIVAL. The carnival still comes to town each July 4th.

THE VILLAGE, 1950. The Village has changed little over the years.

ST. SIMONS VILLAGE. Providing shopping and a place to eat, The Village is still a gathering place and the center of activity on the island.

A "TUG OF WAR" AT EAST BEACH, ST. SIMONS ISLAND, GA.—24

TUG OF WAR, 1950. Today the beach remains as popular as ever.

TOLOMATO GOLF CLUB, SAINT SIMONS ISLAND   BRUNSWICK, GA.

TOLOMATO GOLF CLUB.
For some golf is the favorite
thing to do on the island.
The Tolomato Golf Club,
located on the site of Retreat
Plantation, is now the Sea
Island Golf Club.

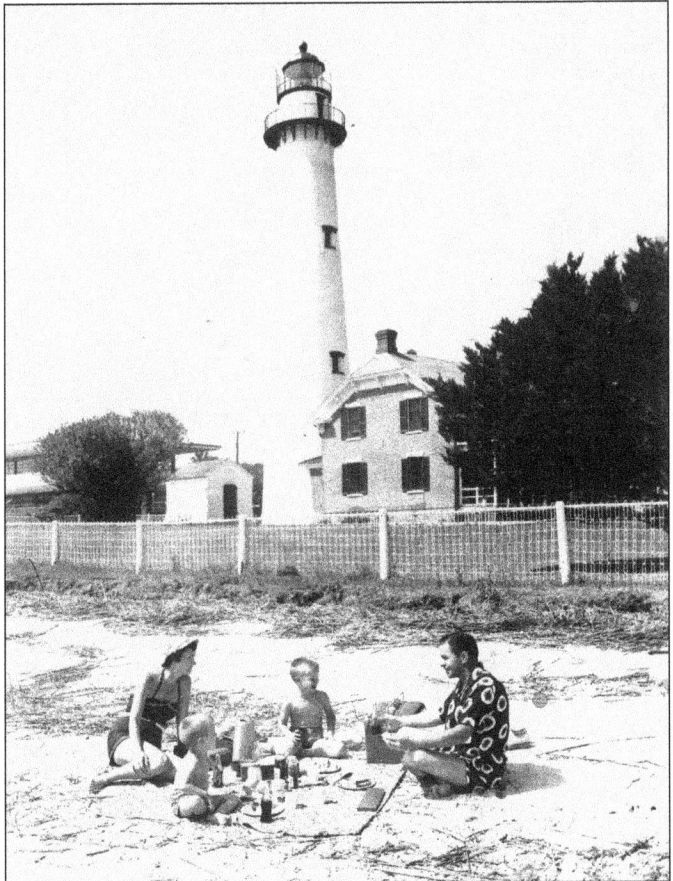

**VANCE SHAEFFER AND
FAMILY, C. 1950.** St. Simons
remains a family place.

LOOKING FROM THE PIER DOWN THE BEACH. St. Simons still remains as a gem along Georgia's coast.